TIME FOR KIDS®

CONFIDENT 3 READER

Science Scoops

SHARKS!

By the Editors of TIME FOR KIDS
WITH ADRIENNE BETZ

HarperCollins*Publishers*

About the Author: Adrienne Betz has been a children's librarian, writer, editor, and consultant for TIME FOR KIDS and other companies. She has written more than sixty nonfiction books for children and loves to write about animals and the people who study them.

To Ben, the greatest first-grade shark expert I ever met.

Thanks to these real experts for sharing their time: Samuel Gruber (Director, Bimini Biological Field Station; University of Miami), John Musick (Virginia Institute of Shark Science), George H. Burgess (Florida Program for Shark Research; Web Editor, International Shark File), Ramón Bonfil (Wildlife Conservation Society), and photographer Jeff Rotman. —A.B.

LIBRARY OF CONGRESS CATALOGING-IN-PUBLICATION DATA

Sharks! / by the editors of Time for Kids with Adrienne Betz.— 1st ed.
p. cm. — (Time for kids science scoops)
ISBN 0-06-057632-4 (pbk.) — ISBN 0-06-057633-2 (trade)
1. Sharks—Juvenile literature. [1. Sharks.] I. Betz, Adrienne. II. Time for kids online.
III. Series.
QL638.9.B48 2005   2003026551
597.3—dc22

1 2 3 4 5 6 7 8 9 10
First Edition

Photography and Illustration Credits:
Cover: Stuart Westmorland—Getty Images; cover inset: Isabelle Delafosse—Jeff Rotman Photography; cover front and back flap: Stephen Frink—Digital Vision; title page: Stephen Frink—Digital Vision; contents page: Stephen Frink—Digital Vision; all borders: Stephen Frink—Digital Vision; pp. 4–5: Digital Vision; pp. 6–7: Taxi/Getty Images; p. 7 (inset): Jeff Rotman; pp. 8–9: Graphic for TIME by Ed Gabel; p. 9 (inset-bottom): Dr. Rocky Strong; pp. 10–11: Jeff Rotman; pp. 12–13: Paul Humann—Seapics.com; p. 12 (inset): Fred Bavendam—Minden; p. 13 (inset-top): Doug Perrine—Seapics.com; p. 13 (inset-bottom): Jeremy Stafford-Deitsch—Seapics.com; pp. 14–15: Doug Perrine—Seapics.com; p. 15 (inset-top): Gwen Lowe—Seapics.com; p. 15 (inset-bottom): Masa Ushioda—Seapics.com; pp. 16–17 (top): Marty Snyderman—Index Stock; pp. 16–17 (bottom-left): Jeff Rotman; pp. 16–17 (bottom-right): Isabelle Delafosse—Jeff Rotman Photography; pp. 18–19: Amos Nachoum—Corbis; pp. 20–21: Jeff Rotman; p. 21 (inset): Amos Nachoum—Corbis; pp. 22–23: Dan Burton—Seapics.com; p. 22 (box): Peter Cade—Getty Images; p. 23 (box): Jeff Rotman; pp. 24–25: Tim Calver; pp. 26–27: Tim Calver; p. 26 (inset): Koji Nakamura—Jeff Rotman Photography; pp. 28–29: Doug Perrine—Seapics.com; p. 30 (top): Bruce Rasner—Jeff Rotman Photography; p. 30 (bottom): Jeff Rotman; p. 31 (inset): Doug Perrine—Seapics.com; p. 31 (inset): Jeff Rotman; p. 32 (top left): Dr. Rocky Strong; p. 32 (bottom left): Stephen Frink—Digital Vision; p. 32 (top right): Stephen Frink—Digital Vision; p. 32 (center right): Koji Nakamura—Jeff Rotman Photography; p. 32 (bottom right): Paul Humann—Seapics.com; back cover: Stephen Frink—Digital Vision

Acknowledgments:
For TIME FOR KIDS: Editorial Director: Keith Garton; Editor: Nelida Gonzalez Cutler; Art Director: Rachel Smith; Photography Editors: Don Heiny and Jill Tatara

go Check us out at **www.timeforkids.com**

CONTENTS

CHAPTER ONE

Here Comes

Whitetip
reef shark

4

a Shark!

This is not just any fish. It's a shark! As it swims, its tail moves from side to side. *Swish! Swish!* This shark is hunting for food.

Swish! Swish!

The shark looks and listens.
It can see well in the blue water. It can hear
well, too. Even if there is a tiny drop of blood
in the water, the shark can smell it.

The shark feels something moving in the water.
Swish! Swish! Swish! The shark swims very fast.

The shark grabs a fish! Now it is time to eat.

Sharks are special.

They are different from other animals, even other fish. Here are some of the things that make sharks special.

EYES: Sharks can see better in dim light than people. Some sharks like bright colors and shiny things. They look for them as they swim.

NOSTRILS: Sharks use these only to smell. Sharks breathe by taking water in through their gills and mouth.

Wow! A great white shark's tooth can be this big!

JAWS AND MOUTH: Sharks' jaws have many rows of teeth. Sharks can have thousands of teeth! They do not use their tongues to taste. They use the skin inside their mouths.

EARS: Sharks' ears are inside their head. Sharks can hear sounds that are faraway.

SKIN: Most fish have smooth scales. Sharks are covered with scales called *denticles*. They look like tiny teeth. Ouch! This skin is so rough that it can scratch.

GILLS: All fish have gills. But only sharks have many gill slits on each side of their head. Sharks can have five, six, or seven pairs of gill slits.

FINS: All sharks have fins. Fins help keep sharks from tipping over as they swim.

TAIL: Sharks can bend and twist their tails. That's because there are no bones in sharks' tails—or anywhere else in sharks' bodies. Instead of bones, sharks have rubbery tissue called *cartilage*. You have cartilage, too—in the tip of your nose, for instance!

This is the cartilage of a shark!

CHAPTER TWO

Meet the Family

There are more than five hundred kinds of sharks. All sharks have denticles, fins, and at least five gill slits on each side of their body. But not all sharks are the same.

Whitetip reef sharks

Many sharks swim alone. Not these!
They swim in a *school*, or group. Can you
guess why they're called hammerheads?

This shark has a flat body and spots. It lives on the ocean floor. That's why it's called a carpet shark. It can use its fins to walk!

This shark is small. But it can gulp down a lot of water. Then it swells up. That's why it's called a swell shark.

This thresher shark has a very long tail.

The thresher shark uses its tail to push little fish toward its mouth.

The dwarf shark is the smallest
shark. It's only six inches long.
It lives in deep, dark waters.
It glows in the dark.

This gentle shark can grow to be bigger than a bus! It's the biggest fish in the sea. That's why it's called a whale shark.

FACE-TO-FACE WITH SHARKS

Jeff Rotman takes pictures of sharks. It's not an easy job! "The hardest part is finding the sharks," says Rotman. He travels all around the world looking for sharks. Whale sharks don't bite people. But other sharks, like these reef sharks, can be dangerous. Rotman always dives with a buddy for greater safety. Rotman wears a special suit. Sharks can't bite through it!

17

CHAPTER THREE

Open Wide!

CHOMP!

What has many teeth but never chews? A shark! This is a great white shark. It uses its teeth to grab and bite. Then it gulps down big chunks of food.

Different kinds of sharks eat different things.

Their teeth are just right for the food they eat. This nurse shark has small teeth. It uses them to crush crab shells. Crab is one of the foods it likes best.

This mako shark is big and strong.
Its teeth are very, very sharp. It hunts for
fish that are even bigger than it is. *Crunch!*

This basking shark is almost as big as a whale shark.

Both whale sharks and basking sharks have a lot of little teeth. Most of the time the sharks do not use their teeth at all. They suck in tiny animals through their gills and mouths.

How Big?

A basking shark's tooth is about one-eighth inch long. That's smaller than one of your baby teeth!

The great white shark has the biggest teeth of any living shark. A tooth can grow to be three inches long.

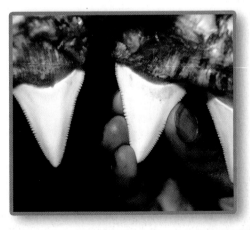

CHAPTER FOUR

Studying Sharks

Do sharks always stay in one place? Or do they travel great distances? Scientists put tags on sharks to find out. The tags send signals back to a receiver. Scientists found that some sharks travel thousands of miles each year.

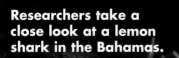

Researchers take a
close look at a lemon
shark in the Bahamas.

Shark babies are called *pups*. They are born with teeth. They can take care of themselves. Some scientists study how shark pups grow.

UNDERSTANDING SHARKS

Dr. Samuel Gruber is a shark scientist. One day when he was swimming, he saw a hammerhead shark. It was coming close! Was it going to attack? No! It just swam away. After that, Gruber knew he wanted to study sharks.

Gruber learned that some sharks like bright orange and yellow. Swimmers should not wear these colors. Gruber studies lemon sharks. He found out that a mother lemon shark swims to a special place to have her pups. The pups stay there for as many as twelve years. Then they swim off into the deep sea. "Sharks almost never attack people," Gruber says. "But people kill millions of sharks each year."

Dr. Samuel Gruber with a lemon shark pup

Scientists say people kill too many sharks.

That is why some countries have laws to limit shark fishing. There is a balance in nature.

Gray reef shark

Some animals eat plants. Some animals, like sharks, eat other animals. If there were no more sharks, the balance would change. Our world needs sharks.

Scientists keep finding new kinds of sharks. This type of huge shark was first seen in 1976. It's called a megamouth.

Did You Know?

◆ Sharks have been around for a long, long time! They were swimming in the sea before dinosaurs walked on the land. These kids are standing inside a model of the jaws of an ancient megalodon shark.

◆ As soon as a shark's tooth falls out, a new one grows in.

◆ Scientists say that some sharks live to be more than one hundred fifty years old.

◆ Most sharks spend about half their time hunting for food. It may take hours for a shark to find a good meal. After a big shark eats, it may not eat again for days!

STAY SAFE!

Sharks usually keep away from people. More people die from bee stings than from shark attacks. Sharks do not think people are very tasty. But sharks that eat turtles or sea lions might snap at a surfer.
Can you see why?

SWIMMING DOS AND DON'TS

◆ Don't swim if you have a cut or are bleeding.

◆ Don't wear anything shiny.

◆ Don't swim alone.

◆ Don't swim from the early evening to the early morning.

If you see a shark, do swim or walk slowly back to shore.

◆ Don't splash or yell.

◆ Do tell other swimmers to get out of the water.

◆ Do tell a grown-up what you saw.

DANGER

WORDS to Know

Cartilage: rubbery tissue; cartilage allows a shark to bend and twist in the water

Gills: organs that allow a fish to breathe by getting oxygen from water

Denticles: the sharp, toothlike scales covering a shark's body

Pup: a shark baby

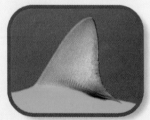

Fins: a part of a fish; the fin on the shark's back keeps it steady as it swims

School: a group of fish swimming together

FUN FACTS — TOP 5 HEAVIEST SHARKS

Sharks come in all sizes. Some sharks are small enough to fit into the palm of your hand. Don't try that with these big fish!

1
Whale shark
46,300 pounds

2
Basking shark
32,000 pounds

3
Great white shark
7,300 pounds

4
Greenland shark
2,250 pounds

5
Tiger shark
2,070 pounds